TIDES AND SEASONS

David Adam is the Vicar of Holy Island. He has a
particular interest in Celtic Christian traditions, of
which he detects traces still lingering in the North-
ern Church. The first collection of his prayers
composed in the Celtic manner, *The Edge of Glory*,
achieved instant popularity. Since then he has also
written *The Cry of the Deer: Meditations on the Hymn of
St Patrick* and *The Eye of the Eagle: Meditations on the
Hymn 'Be thou my vision'*.

TIDES AND SEASONS

DAVID ADAM

Illustrated by
Peter Dingle and Jenny Pearson

TRiANGLE

First published 1989
Triangle
SPCK
Holy Trinity Church
Marylebone Road
London NW1 4DU

Third impression 1991

British Library Cataloguing in Publication Data

Adam, David, 1936–
    Tides and seasons
    1. Christian life Prayers   Devotional works
    I. Title
    242'.8

    ISBN 0-281-04408-2

Typeset by Rowland Phototypesetting Ltd
Bury St Edmunds, Suffolk
Printed in Great Britain by
BPCC Hazell Books
Aylesbury, Bucks, England
Member of BPCC Ltd.

TO JOCK ADAM

My father who made sure of
my Celtic heritage

ACKNOWLEDGEMENTS

I should like to thank Peter Dingle and Jenny Pearson, and also Elisabeth Randles and Denise Adam, for the artwork in this book. These drawings are often not only works of art but meditations in themselves. You cannot look at Celtic art without realising it is for meditation also.

My thanks to Will Taylor for the cover picture.

Many thanks to all who have greatly encouraged me in the ebbing and flowing of life: Danby parish for being willing to share with me this strange movement of tides and the mysteries that surround us; the Ecclesiastical Insurance Office for providing me with a bursary for research; and Denise for her willingness to share all of the Tides and Seasons with me.

Contents

Tides and Seasons

Everything in this life is visited by its tides and seasons. This world is in a state of constant flux; all is flowing, changing. The more alive and alert the creature is, the more likely it is to be changing regularly. All of us are caught up in the pull of the ebb and flow of the whole of creation. In each of us there are many strong currents at work. We are a very small and frail craft in a mighty ocean. Yet we may be privileged to discover, in the ebb and flow, that nothing is lost, only changed. As the tide ebbs on one shore it flows on another. In the ebbing, the sea is not diminished: as one area decreases, another is increasing. The end of one thing always heralds the beginning of something new. In the same way the beginning of something marks the end of an old order.

Within this pattern, we need to see that we are not just a single sequence of tides: we do not begin with the one flowing and end on the ebb. We are more than an ocean with its ebbing and flowing: we contain within ourselves many ebbings and many flowings, many different seas and currents. We are a whole world of tides with many oceans, and at different levels at the same time. In times of diminishment especially, we need to be made aware of other shores, even of eternal reaches. For all of us, as long as we are alive there are always new horizons. In the tenth century Celtic poem, 'The Old Woman of Beare', we see such a tide struggle at work:

> The flood wave
> And the second ebb-tide
> They have reached me.
> I know them well.
> O happy the isle of the great sea
> Which the flood reaches after the ebb!

But ageing and the feeling of guilt or rejection, makes her concentrate on the ebb tide. There is a tendency for all of us to let the world and experience diminish us. The Old Woman of Beare goes on:

> As for me I do not expect
> Flood after ebb to come to me.
> There is scarce a little place today
> That I can recognise:
> What was on flood is all on ebb.

This experience is echoed by most of us more than once in our lives – if not every day! There is a danger at the low ebb to feel we are all alone. Samuel Taylor Coleridge expressed it in his 'Ancient Mariner':

> . . . this soul hath been
> Alone on a wide, wide sea:
> So lonely 'twas, that God himself
> Scarce seemed there to be.

But the Christian does not stop there, even when God seems not to be. We are called to be aware of other tides, other shores. In this world, we are to say like John the Baptist, 'He must increase, I must decrease.' But that is limited to this world and its oceans. We believe in Jesus risen, and the eternal shore

> Where no storms come,
> Where the green swell is in the haven dumb . . .[1]

Or as expressed by a lesser poet, Arthur Clough:

> For while the tired waves, vainly breaking,
> Seemed here no painful inch to gain,
> Far back, through creeks and inlets making
> Comes silent, flooding in, the main.[2]

In this book I have attempted to look at the different tides of life, believing that for most of the time all of the tides are at work in us.

I have chosen the approach of the Celtic Church

because I believe it has a great deal to teach us about the unity of the world and the Divine Presence in it. We are all still close to nature, though many of us are unaware of it, just as many are unaware of its Creator. But both are ever with us. The Celts sought to build an outer world which reflected their belief in the Presence and Oneness of God; a belief well summarised in the words of St Patrick to the princesses of Tara:

> Our God is the God of all men,
> the God of heaven and earth,
> the God of sea, of river, of sun and moon and stars,
> of the lofty mountains and the lowly valleys.
> The God above heaven,
> The God under heaven,
> The God in heaven.
> He has His dwelling round heaven,
> and earth and sea, and all that is in them,
> He inspires all,
> He quickens all,
> He dominates all,
> He sustains all.
> He lights the light of the sun:
> He furnishes the light of light . . .

The Celtic Church saw and reflected a glory which we seem to have lost from the earth. Because of this belief they saw all things inter-related and interdependent. I believe we need to recapture that awareness, for man is not only out of tune with God, he is out of tune with the world and with himself.

In his book *The Tree of Life*, H. J. Massingham wrote:

> If the British Church had survived, it is possible that the fissure between Christianity and nature, widening through the centuries, would not have cracked the unity of western man's attitude to the Universe.[3]

We need, once again, to rediscover the precious links between all living things; that there is a unity at the very heart of our world, and it can be experienced by each of us. Basic to that unity is a combination of God-awareness and what the world now calls ecology.

There is no doubt that we are caught up in cosmic, if not universal tides and seasons. We cannot control them all, nor can we stand apart, but we can seek to be more receptive and aware. We can affirm that we are influencing the whole of our world, as it is influencing us. We can also affirm that God is deeply concerned, for He loves His world. In looking at every tide it might make us face reality a little better. In this world some things do finish, and diminish; but

> . . . For all this, nature is never spent;
> There lives the dearest freshness deep down things;
> And though the last lights off the black West went
> Oh, morning, at the brown brink eastward springs –
> Because the Holy Ghost over the bent
> World broods with warm breast and with ah! bright wings.[4]

INCOMING TIDE

We all experience the incoming tide. We left a world of darkness behind when we arrived on the shore of this world. Our birth was an incoming. Throughout our lives we will again and again be offered new experiences, new chances for change, and renewal. For all of us there will be new people to encounter and new places to visit. At all times there will be the coming of the great Other to us; God is ever coming into our lives. So we need to be aware of the coming and to rejoice in it. We should make sure that our life has a good inflow and is not 'all on ebb'. It is interesting to know that the Aid Woman on the Hebridean islands liked the child to be born if possible on an incoming tide. As soon as possible the child would be dipped in the incoming tide, expressing the simple desire that his or her life would freely flow.

The incoming tide marks the beginning of things, the springtime of our lives. It is necessary to keep a freshness and an openness at all times. The world will flood us with newness each day, we will be offered change and the challenge of change. Most people say they rejoice in the incoming tide, that it is far more acceptable than the outgoing. But, in fact, we all seek to control this tide as much as we seek to control the others. We filter out experiences and avoid certain encounters. There are many worlds about us but we seek to choose one. We allow clouds to gather around us that restrict our vision. This is as true of our material awareness as it is of our vision of God. It is as T. S. Eliot says:

Human kind cannot bear very much reality.[1]

There is a danger that Christians give the impression that they do not love the world, that we should flee from the world. We need to proclaim strongly that it is God's world, that it is basically good, and that God himself loves it. The true monk of the desert never fled the world, only the game of trivial pursuits that so many persist in playing. It is easier to hide from the world in busy streets and air-conditioned offices than it is in the desert. It is harder to hide from the incoming tide when all surrounding cover has been removed. The true monk of the desert sought to enter deeper and deeper into life. This is to be the task of all of us. In *Hymn of the Universe*, Teilhard de Chardin says:

> Purity does not come in separation from but in a deeper penetration into the Universe . . . Bathe yourself in the ocean of matter; plunge into it where it is deepest and most violent; struggle in its currents and drink its waters. For it cradled you long ago in your preconscious existence: and it is the ocean that will raise you up to God.[2]

Let us learn not only to become more aware of what comes to us but to rejoice in it. To know each day that He comes and He seeks to make all things new.

Maker of All

You are the Maker
Of earth and sky,
You are the Maker
Of heaven on high.
You are the Maker
Of oceans deep,
You are the Maker
Of mountains steep.
You are the Maker
Of sun and rain,
You are the Maker
Of hill and plain.
You are the Maker
Of such as me.
Keep me, O Lord
Eternally.

Teach me to see you, Lord,
In all things seen and heard,
In beauty of the heather moors,
In the singing of a bird.

Consecration

Father, bless to me the dawn,
Bless to me the coming morn.
Bless all that my eyes will see.
Bless all that will come to me.
Bless my neighbour and my friend.
Bless until our journey's end.
Bless the traveller to our shore.
Bless the stranger at our door.
Bless to me the opening year.
Bless all who to me are dear.
Bless, O Lord, this day of days.
Bless with riches all our ways.

Awaken me, Lord

Awaken me, Lord
To your light,
Open my eyes
To your presence

Awaken me, Lord
To your love,
Open my heart
To your indwelling.

Awaken me, Lord
To your life,
Open my mind
To your abiding.

Awaken me, Lord
To your purpose,
Open my will
To your guiding.

Rising Prayer

Thanks be to the Father
I arise to today.
He gives me light.
He guides my way.

Thanks be to the Saviour
I arise today.
He gives me love.
He hears me pray.

Thanks be to the Spirit
I arise today.
He gives me life
With me to stay.

Christ Everlasting Friend

Christ in my beginning
Christ there at my end
Christ be in my journey
Christ everlasting friend
Christ be in my waking
Christ at my repose
Christ in every action
Christ when eyelids close

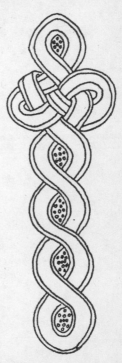

For a New Day

God of Time
God of Space
Fill this moment
With your grace.
God of Motion
God of Peace
From each sin
Give release.
God of Quiet
God of Might
Keep us ever
In your sight.

Dressing Prayer

This day I bind around me
The power of the Sacred Three:
The hand to hold,
The heart to love,
The eye to see,
The Presence of the Trinity.

I wrap around my mortal frame
The power of the Creator's name:
The Father's might, His holy arm,
To shield this day and keep from harm.

I cover myself from above
With the great Redeemer's love.
The Son's bright light to shine on me,
To protect this day, to eternity.

I pull around me with morning light
The knowledge of the Spirit's sight.
The Strengthener's eye to keep guard,
Covering my path when it is hard.

This day I bind around me
The power of the Sacred Three.

Morning Prayer

Lord you are in this place,
        Fill us with your power,
        Cover us with your peace,
        Show us your presence.

Lord help us to know,
        We are in your hands,
        We are under your protection,
        We are covered by your love.

Lord we ask you today,
        To deliver us from evil,
        To guide us in our travels,
        To defend us from all harm.

Lord give us now,
        Eyes to see the invisible,
        Ears to hear your call,
        Hands to do your work,
        And hearts to respond to your love.

Speak, Lord

In the silence of the stars,
In the quiet of the hills,
In the heaving of the sea,
             Speak, Lord.

In the stillness of this room,
In the calming of my mind,
In the longing of my heart,
             Speak, Lord.

In the voice of a friend,
In the chatter of a child,
In the words of a stranger,
             Speak, Lord.

In the opening of a book,
In the looking at a film,
In the listening to music,
             Speak, Lord,

For your servant listens.

Baptism

In my palm the water lies,
A drop for the Creator
Of the skies.

In my palm the water lies
A drop for the Saviour
Who did rise.

In my palm the water lies
A drop for the Spirit
Ever wise.

In my palm the water lies
Drops for the Triune
Who sanctifies.

The Father's love
In your face reflected

The Son's love
Keeping you protected

The Spirit's love
In your life shining

The Triune love
Eternally entwining.

Holy Baptism

In the Father's love,
    the Creator's love,

In the Son's love,
    the Saviour's love,

In the Spirit's love,
    the Strengthener's love,

Three drops of water fall
On your head so small.
A drop to help you walk the earth,
A drop to raise you to the skies,
A drop to show your eternal worth.

Christian babe, now, arise.

Triune Blessing

A drop of water
For you to inherit
Father, Son and Holy Spirit.

A drop of water
Ever so small
The Power of God
To fill you all.
A little washing
Of your face
The Holy Three
Give their grace.
A little drop
Upon your brow
Triune Presence
With you now.

Birth Pangs

Born of fire
Born of sun
Born of moon
There you begun.

Born of stars
Born of earth
Born of soil
Giving you birth.

Born of wind
Born of air
Born of sky
You come from there.

Born of clouds
Born of rain
Born of waters
Your birth pain.

Born of fish
Born of creatures
Born of birds
Your very features.

Born of Father
Born of Son
Born of Spirit
How all begun.

A Genealogy

Son of the elements,
  Son of Vapours
  Son of Wind
  Son of Air.

Son of the elements,
  Son of Light
  Son of Heat
  Son of Fire.

Son of the elements,
  Son of Rain
  Son of Waves
  Son of Water.

Son of the elements,
  Son of Land
  Son of Soil
  Son of Earth.

Son of the elements,
  Son of Stars
  Son of Planets
  Son of Moon.

Son of the elements,
  Son of Creatures
  Son of Man
  Son of God.

Immersion

In the Holy Three
I you immerse
To save you from
Each ill and curse,
That all your life
They are close by
Protecting you still
When you come to die.

In the Power of the Creator,
In the Peace of the Redeemer,
In the Presence of the Spirit,
We welcome you.

Three in your coming
Three with you staying,
Three until your going,
We welcome you.

In the Love of the Father,
In the Joy of the Saviour,
In the Strength of the Spirit,
We welcome you.[3]

God in All

In your walking – God
In your talking – God
In your life – God
In your strife – God
In your seeing – God
In your being – God
In your days – God
In your ways – God
In your night – God
In your plight – God
In your reason – God
In every season – God

With God I'm bound
All around
The Trinity
Circle me.
Father
Profound.
Jesus
Confound.
Spirit
Abound.
With God I'm bound
All around.

Our Dwelling

The earth is your dwelling,
Live in us Lord,
Let us live in you.
Settle in our hearts,
At home in our wills,
At rest in our minds,
At ease in our strength,
That we may reside in peace,
Live in joy,
Abide in love,
And inhabit eternity.

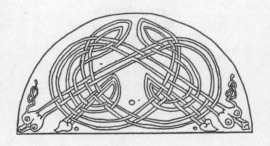

Veni Creator

Come Lord
Come down
Come in
Come among us
Come as the wind
To move us
Come as the light
To prove us
Come as the night
To rest us
Come as the storm
To test us
Come as the sun
To warm us
Come as the stillness
To calm us
Come Lord
Come down
Come in
Come among us.

Be Opened

Lord, open our lips,
And our mouth shall declare your praise.

Lord, open our eyes,
And our seeing shall behold your glory.

Lord, open our hearts,
And our feeling shall know your love.

Lord, open our minds,
And our thinking shall discover your wonders.

Lord, open our hands,
And our giving shall show your generosity.

Lord, open our lives,
And our living shall declare your Presence.

It is the Lord

It is the Lord, in the dawning,
            in the renewal,
            in the arrival,
            in the new day.

It is the Lord, in the crowd,
            in the church,
            in the conversation,
            in the crisis.

It is the Lord, in our joys,
            in our sorrows,
            in our sickness,
            in our health.

It is the Lord, in the stable,
            in the humble,
            in the stranger,
            in the poor.

It is the Lord, risen and returned,
            alive for evermore,
            giving me new life,
            saving me in strife,
                It is the Lord.

With you, Lord

You are to be found in our lives,
Help us to seek you.

You do wonders among us,
Help us to see you.

You reign over our world,
Help us to obey you.

You triumph over all,
Help us to rise with you.

You enter your kingdom,
Help us to live with you.

O Lord, Give Us

O Lord, give us yourself above all things.
It is in your coming alone that we are enriched.
It is in your coming that your true gifts come.
Come, Lord, that we may share the gifts of your
    Presence.
Come, Lord, with healing of the past,
Come and calm our memories,
Come with joy for the present,
Come and give life to our existence,
Come with hope for the future,
Come and give a sense of eternity.
Come with strength for our wills,
Come with power for our thoughts,
Come with love for our heart,
Come and give affection to our being.
Come, Lord, give yourself above all things,
And help us to give ourselves to you.

Glory

Let this day be a day of glory to me.
The glory of Bethlehem,
Your coming to earth.
The glory of Cana,
Your sharing in mirth.
The glory of Galilee,
Your bringing of calm.
The glory of Bethesda,
Your saving from harm.
The glory of Calvary,
Your sacrificial love.
The glory of Easter,
Your rising above.
The glory of Ascension,
Your Presence to see.
Let this day be a day of glory to me.

Lord, lift us up from the earth that we may see your
glory.

I Have Seen the Lord

Where the mist rises from the sea,
Where the waves creep upon the shore,
Where the wrack lifts upon the strand,
        I have seen the Lord.

Where the sun awakens the day,
Where the road winds on its way,
Where the fields are sweet with hay,
        I have seen the Lord.

Where the stars shine in the sky,
Where the streets so peaceful lie,
Where the darkness is so nigh,
        I have seen the Lord.

The Lord is here,
The Lord is there,
The Lord is everywhere.
The Lord is high,
The Lord is low,
The Lord is on the path I go.

Three in One

O mighty God of every place,
O Holy Son of kindly face,
O Spirit God of inner grace,
      Have mercy upon us.

Creator God on You we rely,
Saviour God let us not die,
Spirit God come from on high,
      Have mercy on us.

Three in One of you we are blessed,
One in Three give us your rest,
Trinity God by us confessed,
      Have mercy upon us.

Holy God, make us holy,
Wholesome God make us whole,
Healthy God make us healthy,
Holy, Strong One, God Almighty.

Blessing

I give this blessing
With my hand,
God, Himself,
Before you stand.

I give this blessing
Before you go,
Christ, Himself,
Within you flow.

I give this blessing
Upon all here,
Spirit, Himself,
Be with you near.

I give this blessing
Whoever you be,
God bless you now
And eternally.

Sea Tides

Let the love tide swelling
Surround me and my dwelling.
Let the power of the mighty sea
Flow in, Lord, and strengthen me.
Tide of Christ covering my shore
That I may live for evermore.

Whatever the tide
The Lord at my side,
In storm or in calm
To keep me from harm,
In good or in ill
He's with me still.

Some things in life ebb as others flow,
and some things flow as others ebb.
Lord, let my praises never reach an ebb tide.

In the Beginning, God

Know that at this very moment we dwell in Him, and He in us.
Our beginning and our end are in Him.
In Him we live and move and have our being.
Know that all things have their beginning in Him.

Rest for a few moments knowing the fact that nothing can separate us from the love of God.

PICTURE
Meister Eckhart said, 'Every creature is a word of God and a book about God.'
   Take a piece of creation and start to seek out its beginnings. Take something earthy and discover the mysteries of creation. See if you can visualise how the first drop of water began, or how soil was formed over the earth.
   Picture the beginning of the air we breathe, or the start of a single species of flower. Choose just one thing and probe its depths, its mysteries and its beginnings.
   I seek to meditate every week on a single part of God's creation. Why not do the same?

PONDER
                    Take time to consider that –
                    God is beyond space.
                    God is beyond time.
                    God is beyond matter.
                    God is beyond words.
                    God is beyond understanding.
                    God is beyond our senses.

This is what some people call 'transcendence', the God beyond.
   But God is also IN.

                    In the beginning, God.
                    In the beginning of space.
                    In the beginning of time.
                    In the beginning of matter.
                    In the beginning of our life.
                    In his creation.
                    In the heart of each of us.

32

This is what some people call 'immanence', declaring that God is among us and is to be discovered through His creation.

We can see creation as the first incarnation, where God dwells and it is in God. For us the primary scriptures are creation. God is waiting to be revealed through His world. If we fail to understand His world, or decide that we do not like it, how can we understand or love its Creator?

We must seek God in every beginning, for He is there. We must learn to discover His Presence in each encounter. It is how we begin that will influence how we continue and what we see, so we need to begin with the glory and the Presence. We can discover that the God who is beyond can be comprehended by our love and that love of necessity must begin with His world. Here is part of a sermon by the Celtic monk Columbanus:

Seek no farther concerning God: for those who wish to know the great deep must first review the natural world. For knowledge of the Trinity is properly likened to the depths of the sea, according to the saying of the Sage. And the great deep who can find it out? If then a man wishes to know the deepest ocean of divine understanding, let him first if he is able scan that visible sea, and the less he finds himself able to understand of those creatures which lurk beneath the waves, the more let him realise that he can know less of the depths of its Creator: and as he ought and should, let him venture to treat less of Creator than of creature, since none can be competent in the greater if he has not first explored the less, and when a man is not trusted in the lesser, in the greater how should he be trusted? For why, I ask, does a man ignorant of earthly things examine the heavenly? . . . Understand the creation, if you wish to know the Creator.[4]

So let us make sure that we do just that; let us seek to comprehend with our love even if we cannot with our mind. It is a pity that, when given the privilege of a mystical revelation through creation, most of us just want to make an inventory. We are a consumer society and we consume rather than savour.

'God's goodness fills all His creatures and all His blessed works full and endlessly overflows in them'[5]

That each day you will look at one of God's creatures with love and that you will explore its beginnings.

> All life that is within the sea,
> In river every dwelling thing,
> All in the firmament that be
> Thy goodness overflowing sing,
> O Jesu, Jesu, Jesu,
> Unto whom all praise is due.
>
> Each single star fixed in the sky,
> Each bird arising on the wing,
> They that beneath the sun do lie
> Thy goodness all proclaiming sing,
> O Jesu, Jesu, Jesu,
> Unto whom all praise is due.[6]
>
> O God of the morning, Christ of the hills,
> O Spirit who all the firmament fills,
> O Trinity blest who all goodness wills,
> Keep us all our days.[7]

FULL TIDE

Full Tide

The full tide is the summer of our lives, a time of depth and growth. It is the time when we achieve much and shape who we are. We seek to enjoy life and live it to the full. We will pass exams and pass many milestones. It is a time for stretching and journeying; a time of opportunities and success. We could hardly talk of this tide without remembering the words of Shakespeare:

> There is a tide in the affairs of men,
> Which, taken at the flood, leads on to fortune;
> Omitted, all the voyage of their life
> Is bound in shallows and in miseries.[1]

Yet, we must realise that the flood tide can also overwhelm and destroy. There are lives that let so much flow in that they are unable to accept anything new; people who are always too busy and have no time. There is a great danger of justifying our lives by hyperactivity, or by how much we have amassed. We need to be aware that this tide will turn also; it is just one of many tides. We may be fortunate enough to have a life that is 'all on flood', but one day at last it must ebb. In our very riches we must make space so that we can experience the deeps that are offered to us. At flood time there is a great depth to be explored, not just a surface to be skimmed. We are not called just to be inshore sailors, but to launch out, and to explore the mysteries of the depths. We approach the great mystery of God through the deep mysteries of His creation, through a reverence for and a respect of the world in which we live.

Full tide in particular is a time of love in all its fullness. If we do not love the creation, how can we say we love its Creator? Some good advice on our approach to life in its fullness comes from Dostoevsky in *The Brothers Karamazov*:

> Brothers, do not be afraid of contact with sinful men. Love man even in his sin, for that love is like the divine love – the highest of all. Love all God's creation – the whole of it, every grain of sand. Love every leaf, every ray of light. Love the animals, love the plants, love everything. If you love each thing you will perceive the mystery of God in all. Once you perceive this, you will begin to understand it better every day, and you will come at last to love the whole world with an all-embracing love.
>
> Brothers, love is a great teacher; but we must learn how to acquire it, for it is got with difficulty. We buy it dearly, slowly, and with much labour. Everyone can love occasionally – even the wicked can do that; but we must love not for a moment but for ever.

To me this sounds like good Eastern Orthodox teaching on meditation. It is also very like the approach of the Celtic Church to nature. If you want further guidelines on this way of looking at the world in its flood, you could hardly find better that Ignatius Loyola's 'Contemplation for achieving love':

> See God in his creatures –
> in matter giving it existence,
> in plants giving them life,
> in animals giving them consciousness,
> in men giving them intelligence.
> So He lives in me, giving me existence, life, consciousness, intelligence . . .
>
> Think of God energising, as though He were actually at work, in every created reality, in the sky, in matter, plants and fruits, herds and the like . . .
>
> Realise that all gifts and benefits come from above. My moderate ability comes from the supreme Omnipotence on high, as do my sense of justice,

kindliness, charity, mercy and so on ... like sun-
beams from the sun or streams from their source.[2]

If we are able to begin to approach life like that, we shall
be greatly enriched in the flood tide.

Each Church is Bethlehem

I open the stable door,
I kneel before the infant.
I worship with the shepherds.
I adore the Christ child.
I ponder the Word made flesh.
I absorb the love of God.
I sing Glory with the angels.
I offer my gifts with the Magi.
I have come from lands afar.
I receive the living Lord.
I hold him in my hands.
I go on my way rejoicing.
Glorifying and praising God.

Pathways

Lord, today brings
        Paths to discover
        Possibilities to choose
        People to encounter
        Peace to possess
        Promises to fulfil
        Perplexities to ponder
        Power to strengthen
        Pointers to guide
        Pardon to accept
        Praises to sing
and a Presence to proclaim.

Exposure

Reveal, O Lord, to my eyes your glory.
Expose, O Lord, to my heart your love.
Disperse, O Lord, from my mind the darkness.
Fill, O Lord, my life with your light.
Protect, O Lord, from thoughts without action.
Guard, O Lord, from words without feelings.
Defend, O Lord, from ideas without results.
And surround me with your Presence.
Open my eyes
     my heart
     my mind
     my will
     my soul
To the blowing of your Spirit.

Ebb and Flow

Grant to me, Lord,
Joy in giving,
Joy in receiving.
Love in-coming,
Love out-flowing.
Peace instilling,
Peace distilling.
Wisdom infilling,
Wisdom outpouring.
Grant to me, Lord,
A rhythm of life.

God who my life sanctified
Jesus Christ who death defied
Spirit ever at my side
From inflowing to ebb tide
From ebbing to inflowing tide
Ever with me abide.

Freedom

Lord hear us.
> Forgive our sins.
> Free us from evil.
> Deliver us from bondage.
> Release us from captivity.
>
> Liberate us as people.
> Loose us from convention.
> Unfetter us from habit.
> Save us from worry.
>
> Allow us to travel.
> Feed us in the desert.
> Protect us from hunger.
> Shield us from thirst.
> Shelter us from harm.

'That we may know the glorious liberty of the children of God.'

Jesus is Here

Jesus coming down from heaven,
       come to me.
Jesus born in a stable,
       be born in me.
Jesus accepting the shepherds,
       accept me.
Jesus receiving the Magi,
       receive me.
Jesus dwelling in Nazareth,
       dwell in me.
Jesus abiding with Mary,
       abide with me.
Jesus tempted of Satan,
       deliver me.
Jesus healing the blind,
       give sight to me.
Jesus curing the dumb,
       give speech to me.
Jesus light of the world,
       enlighten me.
Jesus risen from the dead,
       uplift me.

With Us

The Lord is here,
His Spirit is with us.

We need not fear,
His Spirit is with us.

We are surrounded by love,
His Spirit is with us.

We are immersed in peace,
His Spirit is with us.

We rejoice in hope,
His Spirit is with us.

We travel in faith,
His Spirit is with us.

We live in eternity,
His Spirit is with us.

The Lord is in this place,
His Spirit is with us.

Risen Again

Let the earth proclaim
The joy of your Name.

Let each bulb rejoice,
Its growth be a voice.

Let each seed and flower
Tell of your power.

Let the glowing bright sun
Show the deed that is done.

Let us hear from the rain
He is risen again.

Let all repeat the refrain
He is risen again.

Lord of the Elements

Lord of the elements
All praises due.
Lord of the oceans
Glory to you.
You give the morning
And the fresh dew.
You give your Presence
Loyal and true.
You give me life
My being renew.
Lord of the elements
Glory to you.

Glory

Glory in all my seeing
Glory in all my being
Glory in all my speaking
Glory in all my seeking
Glory in all my hearing
Glory in every appearing
Glory in all my feeling
Glory in God's revealing
Glory of the Mighty Three
Glory entwining round me
Glory in the opening day
Glory in the rocky way
Glory in the morning light
Glory in the darkest night
Glory there for beholding
Glory ever me enfolding.

Glory of God
Hand above
Glory of Christ
Heart of love
Glory of Spirit
Covering dove.

Flowing Free

The love of God
Flowing free
The love of God
Flow out through me

The peace of God
Flowing free
The peace of God
Flow out through me

The life of God
Flowing free
The life of God
Flow out through me.

God gives freely to us so that His powers may flow out from us to the world. He who blocks off this free flow is dammed and needs to become open to the mighty rush of the love, peace and very life of God which is ever flowing free.

It is easily possible to add extra verses from the great store of God's gifts to us.

Lead me Lord

Lead me Lord,
> In the paths of peacefulness
> In the roads of righteousness
> In the ways of willingness.

Lead me Lord,
> Down the tracks of thoughtfulness
> In the streets of sensitiveness
> By the journey of joyfulness.

Help us Lord

Help us Lord,
> To live in your light
> To act in your might
> To think in your wisdom
> To walk in your kingdom
> To abide in your love
> Your presence to prove.

Holy Caim

Circle of Witnesses
be wound.[3]
Circle of Apostles
all around.
Circle of Saints
us surround.
Circle of Martyrs
hallowed ground.
Circle of God
love abound.
Circle of Christ
foes confound.
Circle of Spirit
glory crowned.

Father enfolding send
Let love bend
Until journey's end.
Jesus and Spirit friend
Each your enfolding lend.
Trinity the heavens rend
Come at this day's end
Circling me to defend
Surrounding me as a friend.

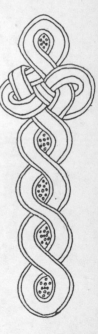

Creator God

What makes the sun to rise?
The power of God.

What makes the seed to grow?
The love of God.

What makes the wind to blow?
The Spirit of God.

Power of God protect us.
Love of God lead us.
Spirit of God strengthen us.
In all of life
And all creation.

Strengthening

I call on strength
From silver moon
I call on strength
From sandy strand
I call on strength
From every rune
I call on strength
From fertile land
I call on strength
From mountain peak
I call on strength
From moorland bleak
I call on strength
From the bright plain
I call on strength
From field of grain
All from the Creator
Near.
All from the Redeemer
Dear.
All from the Spirit
Here.
Providing strength.

Christ the Giver

If Christ be in your heart
Glory fills your days
For He is the King of Glory.

If Christ be in your mind
Peace is in all your ways
For He is the Prince of Peace.

If Christ be in your deeds
Joy your life will raise
For He is the Giver of Joy.

If Christ be in your will
Strength of purpose stays
For He is Sender of Strength.

Jesus Son of Mary

Jesus Son of Mary
       be born in us today.
Jesus lost in the Temple
       seek us when we pray.
Jesus living in Nazareth
       make our house your home.
Jesus in desert tempted
       Forgive us when we roam.
Jesus making water wine
       fill us with your life divine.
Jesus light upon our way
       ever in our darkness shine.
Jesus healer of the sick
       make us strong and whole.
Jesus betrayed, denied
       protect our body and soul.
Jesus upon the cross
       our sure Saviour be.
Jesus risen from the dead
       give us life eternally
Jesus, King, Ascended Lord
       evermore by us adored.

Great High Priest

Christ great High Priest,
Risen on high,
Christ offering life
Never to die.

Christ great High Priest,
Ascended above,
Come down O Lord
Cover with love.

Christ great High Priest,
Back from the dead,
Show us your Presence
In the Bread.

Christ great High Priest
Saviour Divine
Give us yourself
In the red Wine.

My Fortress

God is my fortress
God is my might
God is my Saviour
God is my right
God is my helper
All the day long
God is the Power
Making me strong.

The Captain

Be you my pole star, heavenly guide
Be my sure light over the world wide.
Be you the Captain close at my side
From free-flowing to the ebb tide.

When the storms rage, winds increase,
Draw me Lord to your deep peace.
Be you the Captain close at my side,
From free-flowing to the ebb tide.

If life will ebb or if it will flow,
The Risen Christ with us will go.
Be you the Captain close at my side
From the free-flowing to the ebb tide.

Launch out into the Deep

Use this time to thrust out a little from the land, to discover the amazing depth of the ordinary. Use it until you discover the extra-ordinary that lies in the depths of all things. Realise that you live in the depths all of your life; life is only shallow when we choose to make it so. Move away from what you do out of necessity and habit. Discover the deeps of creation, of your own being, and of God.

PICTURE
See the fishermen mending their nets. Look at the weariness upon them. They are on the beach and their boats are beached also. It as if the tide has left them all behind. Their nets are broken and they have taken them into their hands. Great holes that let life slip through have to be repaired. At the moment it seems that life is escaping from them, slipping through the net and through their fingers. They know it is necessary to make the holes smaller. If the mesh is too large, everything will escape them, so they are mending their nets.

It is at such a moment that He comes. He comes when life seems to be escaping us. He comes when we toil all night and get nothing for it. Beware, He is wanting to cast His net and He is making the casting area smaller. He does not want everyone just to slip away. See Him being jostled by the crowds. The beach is becoming so crowded, He can hardly move. If He is to land a great catch like this He will need help. So He calls to the fishermen. He wants their support. He needs a little space. So He borrows their boat – and the fishermen. For a while the talking goes on but then Jesus comes to the important bit: 'Thrust out a little from the land' – a simple request, but it is the beginning of something bigger. It is nice being there with Him, a bit of time off from work. Sitting there and enjoying the gentle movement of the boat. They begin to wonder why they do not do this more often. It is so relaxing, so refreshing. Because of this action they feel especially close to Him. He is in their boat – and in their lives.

'Launch out into the deep!' That order comes as a bit of a shock. It seems that privileges always bring with them responsibilities. They were just beginning to lie back. 'Launch into the deep!' He wants them to be in the deep waters. He knows that big catches are not in these shallows. 'Launch out into the deep and let down your net for a catch.' Peter wanted to object but he also wanted to plumb new depths, so he obeyed. Here was a catch like never before; though the fishermen were not quite sure who was catching what or whom. All Peter knew was that they had entered the deep with Jesus and their lives would never be the same again. Peter knew that when they came down to earth, when they came to land, they were caught. See what new depths they enter as they leave all behind and follow Him.

PONDER

> Jesus calls us o'er the tumult
> Of our life's wide restless sea.

While we are doing our routine work, He comes.
While we are mending our nets or our cars, He comes.
While the very life we seek is slipping through our fingers,
    He comes.
When we toil all night and catch nothing,
    He comes.
When we are tired and frustrated, He comes.
And every time He comes, He calls.
He calls us today and every day.
'Thrust out a little from the land.' Do not be earth bound, or
    desk bound.

Begin to learn 'the glorious liberty of the children of God'. Move out from the crowd and noise each day, so that you may have a little space around you. So that you may know He is in your boat, your house, your life. If you do not do this, you are hardly ready for the next call, 'Launch out into the deep.' Learn to live in the deep, with a deeper awareness of the world, your neighbour and your God. Of the Celts, Robin Flower wrote:

> It was not only that these scribes and anchorites lived by the destiny of their dedication in an environment of wood and sea; it was because they brought to that environment an eye washed miraculously clear by continuous spiritual exercise that they, first in Europe, had that strange vision of natural things in an almost unnatural purity.[4]

Let us learn to move from the superficial to the deep. Life is not meant to be a perpetual game of trivial pursuits, it is far more glorious than that.

PRAY

> 'Tis God's will I would do,
> My own will I would rein;
> Would give to God his due,
> From my own due refrain;
> God's path I would pursue,
> My own path would disdain.[5]
>
> May God shield us by each sheer drop,
> May Christ keep us on each rock-path,
> May the Spirit fill us on each bare slope,
> as we cross hill and plain,
> Who live and reign
> One God forever. Amen[6]

PROMISE

Promise that each day you will set apart a little time to discover the depths of things, that you will thrust out a little from the land. Seek to enter the depths of Creation that are all around us, that you may see more clearly. Do not be content with the merely superficial.

EBB TIDE

Ebb Tide

The ebb tide is the autumn of life, the season that is also called 'the fall'. It is the time when powers begin to wane, abilities recede, we can fall apart, and some talents even fall off. Ebb tide is often the time of nostalgia, when we look back with fondness, for we are not all that comfortable in the present. The ebb tide feeling is expressed well by Wordsworth in his 'Intimations of Immortality',

> There was a time when meadow, grove, and stream,
> The earth, and every common sight,
>> To me did seem
>> Apparelled in celestial light,
> The glory and the freshness of a dream.
> It is not now as it hath been of yore; –
>> Turn wheresoe'er I may,
>> By night or day,
> The things which I have seen I now can see no more.

This is romantic nostalgia. But we may feel it with great agony of spirit. As the tide ebbs we may discover a great emptiness that nothing we do or say can fill. For many this is a time of troubled spirits. This desperate state is captured by Shakespeare in *Hamlet*

> I have of late – but wherefore I know not – lost all my mirth, forgone all custom of exercise; and indeed it goes so heavily with my disposition that this goodly frame, the earth, seems to me a sterile promontory; this most excellent canopy, the air, look you, this brave o'erhanging firmament, this majestical roof fretted with golden fire, why, it appears no other thing to me but a foul and pestilent congregation of vapours. What a piece of work is man! How noble in reason! how infinite in faculty! in form and moving,

how express and admirable! in action how like an
angel! in apprehension how like a god! the beauty of
the world! the paragon of animals! And yet, to me,
what is this quintessence of dust?'[1]

There is hardly a time like the ebb tide for the question-
ing of life and the feeling that it is quite meaningless. It
is a time that is for most quite frightening and threaten-
ing. A time when we feel alone and often misunder-
stood. It is partly because most people are afraid to
admit that their life ebbs in any way: we all so badly want
to be seen as succeeding and being fulfilled. Yet the
truth is, we all must experience ebb tides if we are to
know the flow. How we deal with them will depend on
our relationship with God. In 1968 the BBC television
produced a song for a series called 'Grief and Glory'
which reflects how alone many feel at the ebb tide:

> Now the earth has put on cold
> And the stars have turned old,
> And man knows how they were made,
> He has grief and glory inside him,
> And he seeks someone to guide him,
> And sings of love unknown.[2]

But for the Christian, hard though this time is, he still
has Glory inside him, he still has Someone to guide
him, he still has a love that is known. Even if in this tide
awareness ebbs, the reality remains. The Presence is
not dependent on our feelings or on our ability. God is
in the ebb as much as the flow. So Alistair Maclean can
write in *Hebridean Altars*:

As the rain hides the stars, as the autumn mists hide
the hills, as the clouds veil the blue of the sky, so the
dark happenings of my lot hide the shining of Thy
face from me. Yet, if I may hold Thy hand in the
darkness, it is enough. Since I know that, though I
may stumble in my going, Thou dost not fall.[3]

Again he writes:

Even though the day be laden and my task dreary and my strength small, a song keeps singing in my heart. For I know that I am Thine. I am part of Thee. Thou art kin to me and all my times are in Thy hand.[4]

This is certainly a time that will put our faith to the test, whatever we have built on. But it is also a time of new opportunities, for it is a time of change. We need to make ourselves aware of what is being revealed on the shore. Our way of life may of necessity change, but we carry within ourselves many riches. Just as the ebb deposits the seaweed on the beaches which it has brought up from the depths, even so out of our deeps new things can be revealed.

If we have lived in awareness of God we may, even at this time, be able to speak boldly, aware that the tide flows elsewhere and that once again it will come flooding in our main. We may even speak the last lines of T. S. Eliot's 'Elder Statesman' with confidence in a loving Father:

Age and decrepitude can have no terrors for me,
Loss and vicissitude cannot appal me,
Not even death can dismay or amaze me
Fixed in the certainty of love unchanging.
                                    I feel utterly secure
In you; I am a part of you. Now take me to my
    father.[5]

In the fall we learn of our frailty, that 'the sea is so large and our boat is so small.' But it can be a time when we awaken our God within us. A time when we learn that 'God so loved the world that He gave His only begotten Son that all who believe in Him should not perish, but have everlasting life.'[6]

Sixfold Kyries

When our days are at their longest
When our life is at its strongest
Kyrie eleison.   Lord have mercy

At the first coming of the dawn
On the life that's newly born
Kyrie eleison.   Lord have mercy

At the turning of each tide
On life's ocean deep and wide
Kyrie eleison.   Lord have mercy

At the ending of the way
At the closing of the day
Kyrie eleison.   Lord have mercy

When our powers are nearly done
At the going down of the sun
Kyrie eleison.   Lord have mercy

When we come to breathe our last
When the gates of death are passed
Kyrie eleison.   Lord have mercy.

The Cross Chases All Evil

I have a charm for a mind confused
I have a charm for a soul that's bruised
I have a charm for a body weary
I have a charm for a spirit dreary
I have a charm for one who is ill
I have a charm to strengthen the will.

The Cross of Jesus

The Cross of Jesus
Bring you balm
The Cross of Jesus
Save from harm
The Cross of Jesus
Soothe your soul
The Cross of Jesus
Keep you whole
The Cross of Jesus
Set you free
The Cross of Jesus
is liberty.

Thoughtfulness

God of love and forgiveness
Save me by your tenderness
From each deed of evilness
From each act of sinfulness
From each thought of carelessness
From each idea of wickedness
From each word of hurtfulness
From each speech of harmfulness
Save me by your tenderness
God of love and forgiveness.

Redeemer

Come Lord and save
> Your creation from evil.
> Your world from corruption.
> Your earth from oppression.

Come Lord and save
> Your children from captivity.
> Your people from injustice.
> Your image from darkness.

Come Lord and save
> Your church from error.
> Your chosen from pride.
> Your Body from dis-ease.

Come Lord and save
> Your loved one from weakness.
> Your dear one from wasting.
> Your redeemed one from death.

Powers of God

Eye of God look upon me
See me in your grace.
Hand of God grasp me
Keep me in my place.
Heart of God love me
Help me to survive.
Powers of God surround me
As with life I strive.

Christ with Us

The Love of Christ
Surround us
The Light of Christ
Lead us
The Peace of Christ
Fill us
The Power of Christ
Aid us
The Joy of Christ
Thrill us
The Presence of Christ
Be with us evermore.

Tides and Seasons

Creator of the tides, give to me
        Space for stillness
        Room for repentance
        Place for prayer
        Home for happiness
        Ways to walk in
        Paths with purpose.

Creator of the seasons, give to me
        Minutes of meditation
        Hours of holiness
        Days of discipline
        Weeks of worship
        Years for you
        Life for love
        Eons of eternity.

Ebb and Flow

From the flowing of the tide
To its ebbing
From the waxing of life
To its waning
Of your Peace provide us
Of your Light lead us
Of your Goodness give us
Of your Grace grant us
Of your Power protect us
Of your Love lift us
And in your Arms accept us
From the ebbing of the tide
To its flowing
From the waning of life
To its waxing

The Great I Am

Jesus the Saviour, save me from sin.
Jesus the Way, watch, warn, walk with me.
Jesus the Truth, teach, tell, transfigure me.
Jesus the Life, lead, lighten, love me.
Jesus the Shepherd, seek, strengthen, save me.
Jesus the Door, direct, draw, deliver me.
Jesus my Peace, pity, pardon, purify me.
Jesus Risen, revive, recreate, renew me.

The Lord

We confess you as King
We accept you as Lord
We offer you our service
We yield you our obedience
We own you as Master
We give you our love
We proffer you our hopes
We tender you our faith
We surrender you our lives.

Lord give yourself to us.

Help in Trouble

Lord you are a present help in trouble.
Come revive
Redeem
Restore
In our darkness come as light
In our sadness come as joy
In our troubles come as peace
In our weakness come as strength
Come Lord to our aid
Revive
Redeem
Restore us

O Lord
        Open our eyes to your Presence
        Open our minds to your grace
        Open our lips to your praises
        Open our hearts to your love
        Open our lives to your healing
        And be found among us.

Grace

Lord you are

       Grace for our needs
       Strength for our weakness
       Light for our blindness
       Love for our loneliness
       Word for our deafness
       Joy for our weariness
       Peace for our anxiousness
       Wonder for our dullness
       Saviour for our hopelessness

Lord you are

       Grace for our needs.

Kyries

Lord have mercy
        On your creation,
        On the world you have made,
        On every living creature,
        On me.
                Lord have mercy

Christ have mercy
        On your salvation,
        On those who are lost,
        On those who stray,
        On me.
                Christ have mercy

Lord have mercy
        On the de-spirited,
        On the depressed,
        On the despairing,
        On me.
                Lord have mercy

Have Mercy

Lord of space
Lord of time
Lord of life
       Have mercy.

God of sun
God of stars
God of earth
       Have mercy.

Jesus of Mary
Jesus of Nazareth
Jesus of Gethsemane
       Have mercy.

Christ of cross
Christ of tomb
Christ risen
       Have mercy.

Spirit on high
Spirit nearby
Spirit of calm
       Have mercy.

Spirit of grace
Spirit of talents
Spirit of life
       Have mercy.

Revelations

Reveal in us your glory
Stir in us your power
Renew in us your kingdom
Develop in us your faith
Show in us your way
Open in us your love
Strengthen in us your hope
Work in us your miracles
Revive in us your resurrection
Abide in us yourself

Giver of My Peace

Giver of my peace
Keep me at morning
Keep me at noon
Keep me at night
Giver of my peace.

Calmer of my strife
Keep me at morning
Keep me at noon
Keep me at night
Calmer of my strife.

Restorer of my life
Keep me at morning
Keep me at noon
Keep me at night
Restorer of my life.

Messiah

To prisoners – freedom
To the blind – sight
To the dumb – the Word
To the lame – the Way
To the sick – health
To the sorrowing – joy
To the despairing – hope
To the troubled – peace
To the poor – riches
To the dead – life
To me – Saviour

Fear not, I am with you; be not dismayed, for I am your God. I will strengthen you, yes I will help you . . . I will uphold you with the right hand of my righteousness.[7]

The Runes

Back and forth, to and fro,
In and out, ebb and flow.
In the Name of the Triune
I make this sacred rune.

In the Name of the Father, Creator He,
Maker of all, in land and sea.

In the Name of Christ upon the Cross
Redeeming mankind, accepting loss.

In the Name of the Spirit, God of power
Protecting each of us every hour.

Back and forth, to and fro,
In and out, ebb and flow.
In the Name of the Triune,
I make this sacred rune.

Power Supplies

God of wind
God of rain
God of sun
God of main
God of moon
God of skies
God of earth
Power supplies.

As I have come to this day,
Bless my life as it ebbs away.

Unending Peace

Take me, Lord, from busy-ness
To the place of quietness
From the tumult without cease
Into your great unending peace.
Help me then, my Lord, to see
What I am and ought to be.

God of life
God of peace
God of wonders
That will not cease
God eternal
Trinity
God everlasting
Come to me.

The Peace of Quiet Hours

The peace of quiet hours
The peace of mighty powers
The peace of the rising sun
The peace of the day that's done
The peace of the deepest sea
The peace of God's prosperity
The peace of God dwelling in you
The peace of Christ and Spirit too.

Mighty Father
In times of stress
Grant us your peacefulness.
In times of weakness
Grant us your forcefulness.
In times of distress
Grant us your hopefulness
In times of sadness
Grant us your joyfulness
And give us awareness.

Caim

When foes confound,
Lord, surround.
When I am afraid,
Lord, your aid.
When at a loss,
Your saving cross.
When storms increase,
Lord, your peace.
When dark's the night,
Lord, be you my light.
And so may it be
Surrounding me
Into eternity.
And so may it be
Surrounding me
Into eternity.

And With Your Spirit

The Lord be with you.
And with your spirit too.

Today, tonight,
In shade and light,
The Lord be with you.
And with your spirit too.

In weakness and pain,
In powers that wane,
The Lord be with you.
And with your spirit too.

In health and in might,
In strength for the fight,
The Lord be with you.
And with your spirit too.

In your coming to rest,
In rising with the blessed,
The Lord be with you.
And with your spirit too.

Powerful Hand

O powerful hand grant (me)
Your might.
O guiding hand grant (me)
Your light.
O healing hand grant (me)
Your balm.
O saving hand grant (me)
Your calm.
O loving hand grant (me)
Your peace.
O redeeming hand grant (me)
Your release.

Going and Coming

God be with my going out,
God be with my coming in,
God be with me in my doubt,
God protecting me from sin.

Christ be with my ebbing,
Christ be with my flowing,
Christ be with my entering,
Christ in love bestowing.

Spirit with me every hour,
Spirit at the journey's end,
Spirit be my every power,
Spirit dove on me descend.

Until the Tide Turns

Lord,
I wait for the tide to turn
Until the distant becomes close,
Until the far off becomes near,
Until the outside is within,
Until the ebb flows.

Lord,
I wait for the tide to turn
Until weakness is made strong,
Until blindness turns to sight,
Until the fractured is made whole,
Until the ebb flows.

Lord,
I wait until the tide turns,
Until the ordinary becomes strange,
Until the empty is Presence-full,
Until the two become one.
Until the ebb flows.

In the Presence of God. Know that you are never alone, that He is always with you. Stop your busy-ness and your struggles to know that He is there. Hear Him say, 'Be still, and know that I am God.' Perhaps you have never really called on Him before: stop all that you are doing, even reading this, and do so now. Know that we cannot survive this life alone, and call upon Him. Take time to realise that amidst the storms of life He is with you. He never leaves you. Relax, knowing He is there. No need for effort to bring Him. Just call upon Him and awaken Him.

You are with Him in this place where you are, and He is with you.

Call upon Him. Say:

> You, Lord, are in my life
> Your Presence fills it
> Your Presence is Peace.

> You Lord are in the Storm
> Your Presence fills it
> Your Presence is Peace.[8]

Know that in this frail craft which we call 'life', He is present.

Picture the disciples in their boat. The day started off well: there were crowds of people clamouring to see Jesus, bringing their troubles for His healing, their anxieties for His calming. The sky was blue and the water like a mill pond. Everything in the world seemed lovely. A good day to be alive. They move away from the crowds and on to the sea. They are tired after a busy day, everyone wants a rest. The gentle rocking of the boat and the lapping of the waters soon have them all resting. Jesus is now asleep in the boat.

What happens next takes them all by surprise, even the seasoned fishermen. A storm hits the boat. Great winds have come from nowhere. The waves rise and dark clouds lower. At first it is just spray that prevents them from seeing clearly, then great waves beat against and enter their boat. They are being driven further and further from the shore and from the area that they know well. They are alone and so small, the sea so large. They are so frail, the waves so mighty and strong. Soon they will be overwhelmed: soon they will perish. Meanwhile, Jesus sleeps in the boat.

Yes, Jesus is there. He has not saved them from the storm. He is there with them in the storm and this will not be the last time. He is there to be called upon. There to be awakened. Yet the disciples try everything they can – to no avail. Soon, it seems, human frailty will be swamped – so they cry out, 'Lord save us, we are perishing!' It will not be the last time they feel like this. The storm is raging about them, they and their vessel are so fragile. Jesus then awakens. He stands amidst the wind and waves, He is there in the storms of life, and He says, 'Peace, be still,' He stills the noise of the waves, the raging of the wind, and the mounting fears of the disciples. They may be now entering a strange country, but they have a new-found peace; for a little while all around them is calm. They are still learning that 'God so loved the world that He gave his only begotten Son, that we should not perish, but have everlasting life.'

PONDER

Think about these words of Julian of Norwich:

> He did not say, 'You shall not be tempest-tossed,
> you shall not be weary,
> you shall not be discomforted.'
> But He said, 'You shall not be overcome.'

Once we believe in Jesus, we do not escape the storms and troubles of life. In fact, in some strange sense more storms than ever seem to come our way. Perhaps we should expect this. If there is any power of evil in the world, we should expect it to oppose anything or anyone that is trying to do what is right and good. However, all of us will meet with storms; there will be times when the tide ebbs on us and we know our human frailty. For all of us will come the experience that we are 'perishing', no matter how far we try and run from it or hide. But for all this God loves and God cares. And there is more. He has sent His Son that we should not perish. In this frail craft that we call life He is present, just waiting to be awakened. Let us learn to call upon Him. Our lives are often like a little boat on a great and stormy sea. It is expressed well by the Hebridean saying;

> So frail our boat, so great yon sea.

Know that we are never left alone, and He does not want us to be overcome.

Here is a prayer thought from the Hebrides:

> Round our skiff be God's aboutness
> Ere she try the deeps of sea,
> Sea-shell frail for all her stoutness
> Unless Thou her Helmsman be.[9]

The following prayer could have been known by the early Celts, and loved by the people that live so close to the sea in all its moods. It is by St Augustine:

> Blessed are all your saints, O God and King, who have travelled over the tempestuous sea of this life and have made the harbour of peace and felicity. Watch over us who are still on this dangerous voyage. Frail is our vessel, and the ocean wide: but as in your mercy you have set our course, so pilot the vessel of our life towards the everlasting shore of peace, and bring us at last to the quiet haven of our heart's desire; through Jesus Christ our Lord. Amen.

From the Book of Common Prayer:

> Keep we beseech thee, O Lord, thy Church with thy perpetual mercy; and because the frailty of man without thee cannot but fall, keep us ever by thy help from all things hurtful, and lead us to all things profitable to our salvation; through Jesus Christ our Lord. Amen.[10]

PROMISE
To call upon the Presence regularly, especially when powers ebb or storms increase. Learn to say regularly:

> Lord, save us, we are perishing.

LOW TIDE

Low Tide

The low tide is the winter of our lives; it is a time of bareness and death. Yet it is also a time of strange beauty, a time of purity – and purifying. In winter we see things that we have never seen before. Our vision on clear days seems lengthened – we can see past the trees also, because the foliage is gone. On the shore, low tide can be a very interesting time. We discover creatures from the deep left by the tide, we visit rocky pools, or ponder over strange fossils in the rocks. On some beaches the shore seems to stretch for miles, as far as the eye can see. We know also that there are other shores and other climes.

D. H. Lawrence, thinking towards death in a poem called 'Shadows', has written this:

> And if tonight my soul may find her peace
> in sleep, and sink in good oblivion,
> and in the morning wake like a new-opened flower
> then I have been dipped again in God, and
>   new-created. . . .
>
> And if in the changing phases of man's life
> I fall in sickness and in misery
> my wrists seem broken and my heart seems dead
> and strength is gone, and my life
> is only the leavings of a life:
>
> And still among it all, snatches of lovely oblivion,
>   and snatches of renewal
> odd wintry flowers upon the withered stem, yet
>   new, strange flowers
> such as my life has not brought forth before, new
>   blossoms of me
>
> then I must know that still
> I am in the hands of the unknown God,
> he is breaking me down to his own oblivion
> to send me forth on a new morning, a new man.[1]

Still, it would be false to make death seem something longed for and beautiful for us all. Most of us would find it hard to say with St Francis:

Praised be my Lord for our sister, bodily death,
From which no man living can flee.

Yet Francis could say it because he was personally sure that the tide would turn. He lived with a confidence in the love of God, and that there is an eternal shore. That is how the famous prayer that bears his name says, 'It is in dying that we are born to eternal life.' It may be that we do not feel so sure or so brave as St Francis. For most, death is a terrible threat to their existence – as are the many deaths that the flesh is heir to. It is certainly a time when we need to know where our real strength comes from. I find in David Gascoyne's 'Fragments towards a *religio poetae*,' an inspiration whenever I am faced by the low tides of this world.

Always, whenever, whatever, however,
When I am able to resist
For once the constant pressure of failure to exist,
Let me remember
That truly to be man is to be man aware of Thee
And unafraid to be. So help me God.[2]

Winter is a time when we need extra protection so that we do not perish. In my part of the world, it is a time when the shepherd will bring his sheep 'in-by'. He brings them off the dangerous and inhospitable hill slopes, away from the storms and the bareness, in-by, where he can give them his attention and look after them. I often make it my prayer that when the great winter storms come, I may also be called in-by into the Presence of the Father.

Winter is a time when we need extra cover, we pull our coats about us. In the time of low tide or of danger, the Hebridean Celts drew round themselves and their loved ones the *caim*. Using the index finger of their

104

right hand they would point and turn a full circle sun-wise; going in this direction was called *deasil* from *dess* meaning right hand. This was no magic, it was no attempt to manipulate God. It was a reminder by action that we are always surrounded by God, He is our encompasser, our encircler. It is our wavering that has put us out of tune. This is a tuning in to the fact that, 'in Him we live and move and have our being'; we are enfolded in Him. The *caim* is a form of praying that I am particularly fond of and recommend you to practise it in troubles, or in fact at any time. Point with your finger, make the circle and say one of the *caim* prayers from this book. Here is another such prayer:

> The Sacred Three
> My fortress be
> Encircling me
> Come and be round
> My hearth my home.[3]

Remember, it is not making something happen, it is an attempt to make us aware of a reality. On the island of Barra an old dame said, 'In such a peril draw the *caim* about thee, and thou art in a fortress.'[4]

Let us at least seek a similar confidence at the low tide. When all about us is changing, let us seek to put our trust in the Almighty God who never changes or falters in His love. Our faith may be small and weak, but it is in a great and mighty God. The tides may wax and wane, life may ebb and flow, but our God remains and He offers us other shores.

> Thou hast destined us for change, us and all things Thy hands have made. Yet we fear not, Nay, rather, we are jubilant. Hast Thou not loved us before the world began? What can change bring us but some better thing?[5]

The Cross of Christ

The Cross of Christ
Upon your brow
The Cross of Christ
Protect you now

The Cross of Christ
Upon your mind
The Cross of Christ
Make you kind

The Cross of Christ
Upon your head
The Cross of Christ
Save from dread

The Cross of Christ
Upon your face
The Cross of Christ
Give you grace

The Cross of Christ
Upon your heart
The Cross of Christ
Set you apart

The Cross of Christ
Upon your soul
The Cross of Christ
Keep you whole

Jesus Lives

In light defeating darkness,
In wisdom conquering foolishness,
In trust overcoming fearfulness,
        Jesus Lives.

In strength coming to weakness,
In health rescuing from sickness,
In hope saving from despair,
        Jesus Lives.

In love victorious over hatred,
In forgiveness dispelling anger,
In glory dispersing drabness,
        Jesus Lives.

In joy growing from sorrow,
In life rising from death,
In God giving the victory,
        Jesus Lives.

He holds the keys of love
        of peace
He holds the keys of life
        of death
He holds the keys of heaven
        of earth
He holds the keys of now
        of eternity.

God Between

Be the strength of God
Between me and each weakness
Be the light of God
Between me and each darkness
Be the joy of God
Between me and each sadness
Be the calm of God
Between me and each madness
Be the life of God
Between me and each death
Be the Spirit of God
Between me and each breath
Be the love of God
Between me and each sigh
Be the Presence of God
With me when I die.

Nunc Dimitis

The day ends, darkness descends,
Now Lord let troubles cease,
Let your servant depart in peace.
Labours are over, my task here done,
Now Lord your victory be won.

Lord when everything trembles
Give me a firm foundation;
Faith founded on facts
Prayers founded on your Presence
Life founded on your love
Peace founded on your power.

Your Presence

Grant me your Presence
In my gasping breath.
Grant me your Presence
In the hour of death.
Grant me your Presence
In my great agony.
Grant me your Presence
Through to eternity.
Grant me your Presence
At the last dark deep.
Grant me your Presence
At the final sleep.
Grant me your Presence
At the long sigh.
Grant me your Presence
Till I come on high.
Grant me your Presence
When the world is past.
Grant me your Presence
When I rest at last.

Caim

The Holy Three
Protecting be
Enfolding me
In eternity
To shield
To save
To circle
To surround
My house
My home
My work
My play
Each night
Each day
Each dark
Each bright
In your light
Forever
May it be
Now
And in eternity.

Lord, Save

From storms of the night
From dark ocean's wave
From the billowing crest
From the watery grave
Save us, Lord, save.

From tempests that roar
From the hurricane's rave
From the rock-strewn shore
From things that deprave
Save us, Lord, save.

Powers of God

The arm of God
Circle about
The arm of God
Put foes to rout.

The love of Christ
Encompassing me
The love of Christ
Setting me free.

The power of Spirit
Now to surround
The power of Spirit
Within me resound.

Lift Us Lord

Into the stormy sea
You descended and lifted Peter.

Into the storms of sickness
You descended and lifted Jairus's daughter.

Into the storms of madness
You descended and lifted Legion.

Into the storms of death
You descended and lifted Lazarus.

Into the storms of hell
You descended and lifted us all.

Lift us Lord,
   From darkness to light
   From sickness to health
   From distress to calm.

Lift us Lord,
   From sadness to joy
   From fear to faith
   From loneliness to love.

Lift us Lord,
   In mind and in spirit
   In word and in deed
   In body and in soul.

Come, Creator

From chaos and emptiness,
From loneliness and lifelessness,
          Come, Creator, Come.

From darkness and shapelessness,
From the abyss and awfulness,
          Come, Creator, Come

From fearfulness and hopelessness,
From weakness and dreadfulness,
          Come, Creator, Come.

The Goal

With God to find hopefulness
In the land beyond all stress,
In the place of gentleness,
Where He will your soul caress,
Where there is new liveliness,
Where the Father will you bless.

May the hills be gentle,
May the valleys be bright,
May the sun shine upon you,
May the moon in the night,
Until your pilgriming soul
Comes to its eternal goal.

To Eternity

Where does the journey end?
Beyond where you can see.

Where do the years end?
That's unknown to you or me.

Where does life end?
In love and eternity.

Enfolding

The Sacred Three
My force field be
Surrounding me
On land or sea.
Defend my kin
Keep peace within
Let darkness cease
Till soul's release.
The Sacred Three
My force field be
Ever to eternity
God enfolding me
On land or sea.

Father, I am lost and lonely.
Hold me with your hand
Guide me by your grace
Lift me by your might
Save me by your strength
Enfold me in your love.

Love Remains Eternally

As in the past
It is now
It will last
It will grow
It will be
To eternity
The Love of God.
May it be so
In ebb and flow,
May it remain
In wax and wane,
The Love of God
It shall be
To eternity.

Father attend
Jesus befriend
Spirit defend
By sea
By shore
Evermore
By land
By sea
Let it be
Evermore
Let it be
Eternally.

The Weaver

I weave into my life this day
The Presence of God upon my way,
I weave into my life this hour
The mighty God and all his power.
I weave into my sore distress
His peace and calm and no less.
I weave into my step so lame
Healing and helping of His name.
I weave into the darkest night
Strands of God shining bright,
I weave into each deed done
Joy and hope of the Risen Son.

Weaving

I weave tonight
A Presence bright
I weave tonight
The sacred Light
Warp on woof.

I weave tonight
The Father's might
I weave tonight
The Saviour's fight
Warp on woof.

I weave tonight
In Spirit's sight
I weave tonight
The Triune right
Warp on woof.

Desert Waters

O spring in the desert
O shelter from the heat
O light in the darkness
O guide for the feet
O joy in our sadness
O support for the weak
O Lord with us always
Your Presence we seek.

God with Us

Father abide
Christ beside
Spirit reside
The Three shield
From hate
From harm
From death's alarm.

Lord be with . . .
In their weakness
Be their strength
In their troubles
Be their peace
In their danger
Be their shelter
In their fears
Be their hope
And be with them evermore.

Jesus Saviour

Jesus, Saviour, Son of God,
Have mercy upon us.

Jesus, Saviour, Son of God,
Grant us your peace.

Jesus, Saviour, Son of God,
Lighten our darkness.

Jesus, Saviour, Son of God,
Deliver us from evil.

Jesus, Saviour, Son of God
Strengthen us for service.

Jesus, Saviour, Son of God,
Abide with us towards evening.

Jesus, Saviour, Son of God,
Keep us in life eternal.

Breath of God

Breath of God inspire us,
        Renew our faith
        Restore our vision
        Revive our love.

Breath of God inspire us,
        Replace our sorrow
        Relieve our sins
        Redeem our situation.

Breath of God inspire us,
        Repair our broken-ness
        Recover our nakedness
        Resurrect our deadness

Breath of God come,
        Refresh
        Redeem
        Restore us.

Caim Rune

This is the prayer
I make today
This is the rune
I wish to say
The Presence of God
To you abound
The Power of God
Keep you sound
The Love of God
Encircle round
The Peace of God
Your life surround
This is the rune
I wish to say
This is the prayer
I make today.

In the Father's way
In Son's bright ray
In the Spirit's sway
Be this day

In the Father's sight
In the Son's light
In the Spirit's might
Be this night

The Shield

The shield of the Father
Covering, caring
From evil's snaring
The shield of the Son
New life supplying
Defence against dying
The shield of the Spirit
A shelter discover
Where we can recover
The shield of the Three
For body and soul
The shield of the Three
Keeping us whole.

Gloria

Awaken us to your glory
Dispel the darkness of night
Destroy the heaviness of heart
Cure the blindness of sight
Heal the deafness of ears
Open the mouth that is dumb
Restore a gentleness of touch
Encourage a sense of adventure
Bring us an awareness of you
Awaken us to your glory.

In working hands
Glory
To the Father.

In words of mouth
Glory
To the Saviour.

In thoughts of hearts
Glory
To the Spirit.

Glory Three
Glory One
Glory evermore
Amen.

The Gate of Glory

Lord,
　　When our steps are weary
　　And the going is rough
　　When our life is dreary
　　And our journey is tough
　　　　　Open the gate of glory

Lord,
　　When the dark clouds thicken
　　And the storm rides high
　　When the troubles quicken
　　And danger is nigh
　　　　　Open the gate of glory

Lord,
　　When our work is completed
　　And the battle is done
　　We are not defeated
　　The victory you have won.
　　　　　Open the gate of glory

Blessings

God's own Presence with you stay
Jesus to shield you in the fray
Spirit to protect you from ill
Trinity there guiding you still.

On sea or land, in ebb or flow
God be with you where you go.
In flow or ebb, on land or sea
God's might your protecting be.

In the Power of the Father on high
In the Peace of the Saviour near by
In the Prosperity of the Spirit stay
The Three enfold you now and away.

God of life
Be with you
God of love
Protect you
God of light
You ensue
Each day
Each night
Each day
Each night.

Your Tide

It is your tide that pulls me Lord,
Draw me to yourself.

When one tide ebbs another flows.
Nothing is lost, only it suffers a tide change.

Lord of life when the tides wane
Grant me a hand till I rise again.
When the strand is becoming wide
Keep me safe at the ebb tide.

You are Risen

You are risen,
Let trumpets proclaim.
You are risen,
Let sun brightly flame.
You are risen
Dark night is past.
You are risen
Hope will now last.
You are risen.
Let us not dread.
You are risen
Back from the dead.
You are risen
Lord of the skies,
You are risen
Help us to rise.

And Jesus Stood on the Shore

Ebb tide, full tide
Over the ocean's rim
Ebb tide, full tide
I travel on with Him.

Full tide, ebb tide
My boat is in the storm.
Full tide, ebb tide
I can see His form.

Ebb tide, full tide
My life is all afloat.
Ebb tide, full tide
He is in my boat.

Full tide, ebb tide
When life is no more
Full tide, ebb tide
He calls me from the shore.

Jesus Stood on the Shore

When morning was come
Jesus stood on the shore.[6]

PAUSE

Do you ever feel that you have spent all your energy for
nothing, that you have worked hard for little or no reward?
Perhaps the light has gone out of your life, you are lonely and
in the dark. This feeling was expressed fully by a couple on
holiday. They had walked down the very steep bank of a
seaside village and back up again; they were weary and felt
frustrated.

'All that walk for nothing,' said the man, gasping for breath.

'All the journey for nothing,' said the woman, almost in
tears.

'That's life', said the man as they travelled on in their trivial
pursuits.

Every now and again it is as if some great tide has ebbed and
we are once more at a low.

This low tide is expressed in many different ways in history
and often by the poets. Here is a piece from an Anglo-Saxon
poem called 'The Seafarer':

He who lives most prosperously on land does not understand how I, careworn and cut off from my kinsmen, have as
an exile endured a winter on the icy sea.[7]

Then again those lines from the 'Ancient Mariner':

. . . this soul hath been
Alone on a wide, wide sea;
So lonely 'twas, that God himself
Scarce seemed there to be.

Certainly the Psalmist was right: *Nisi Dominus frustra*, Without the Lord all frustrates. It is as if some great ebb tide was
determined to strip every thing bare.

PICTURE

So it was with the disciples; they had toiled all night and taken
nothing. Try and see them in the dark, frustrated. They had
travelled for three years with Jesus, expecting a new occupa-

134

tion. Here they were back fishing, back in the dark. They were working hard but achieving nothing. It is not difficult to visualise this situation. Not only nets, but life, seemed empty. There was the nagging feeling that the dull preacher was right when he said, 'Vanity, vanity, all is in vain.' What a way to end their days, toiling in the dark!

Picture it well; you have been there before and will be there again. Life has a habit of suddenly ebbing and laying life bare. There is a feeling, for some of the disciples at least, that they have been here before. This is not an experience that is uncommon to them. This emptiness reverberates with other times, life seems to be repeating itself. Picture them there in the dark, weary, catching nothing. Then watch the dawn come. Even now the tide is flowing on another shore. Picture the bareness being covered, the emptiness being filled. Learn to anticipate and to wait. Know that morning will come.

When morning was come, Jesus stood on the shore.

The dawn has a habit of coming suddenly – though some will aver that 'the darkest moments come just before the dawn.' Picture the disciples suddenly being flooded with light, the sky is blue and the day is bright. The mists are rising on the shore – and there He is, part hidden, wrapped in the morning mist. It would be easy not to notice Him, but He is there.

Jesus stands on the shore waiting for us to come to Him, gently beckoning to us. He calls us through our darkness and frustrations. The low tide reveals the shore – and Jesus standing there. The disciples enter a new day, new life, and new opportunities with their Lord.

PRESENCE
Know that He is there in your darkness.

Know that, though the mists hide Him, he stands waiting on the shore and that He is gently calling you. Say:

> You Lord are in this place
> Your Presence fills it
> Your Presence is light.

In His Presence know that the darkness rolls away. There is a great brightness seeking to enter our lives. Will we still cling to the shadows? Are we determined to stay in the dark? The sun is rising, 'new perils past, new sins forgiven, new thoughts of God, new hopes of heaven'.

See that He is with you. Even when the tide has ebbed Jesus can be found on the shore. When resources are low, renewal is still being offered us. Somewhere within our darkness a brighter dawn seeks to break. Are we able to open our eyes and our minds to the Presence? He is there, where the water meets the land, where the land meets the skies, where the darkness is turning to light, where the temporal is becoming eternal. He is there at each meeting place, every shore of this world – and the shores of eternity.

Even now He waits on you to recognise Him.

He waits on you to turn to Him.

He waits for the darkness to clear and the mists to lift.

He bids us come.

Be refreshed.

Renewed.

Restored.

Lord, open my eyes that I may see – your Presence now and eternally.

PONDER

Think upon these words from Alistair Maclean's *Hebridean Altars*:

> I say to myself each night, 'The dawn will come and all this dark will be gone.' I watch the tide's far ebb and whisper, 'It will flow.' In the mid of winter I cry to my heart, 'Soon the green banners of spring will blow through the land.' Yet surer still I am that Thou art my friend. For Thou hast wrought a miracle in my thought. Thou has changed faith to knowledge, and hope to sight[8]

Also think upon and pray these words from the same book:

Though the dawn breaks cheerless on this Isle today,
my spirit walks upon a path of light.
For I know my greatness
Thou hast built a throne within Thy heart.
I dwell safely within the circle of Thy care.
I cannot for a moment fall out of Thine everlasting arm:
I am on my way to Thy glory.[9]

Saviour and Friend, how wonderful art Thou!
My companion upon the changeful way,
The comforter of its weariness,
My guide to the Eternal Town,
The welcome at its gate.[10]

When the tides of the mind do cease
Let us come, Lord, to your peace.
When the waves rage on no more,
Let us come, Lord, to your shore.

Lighten our darkness, we beseech thee, O Lord; and by thy
great mercy defend us from all perils and dangers of this
night; for the love of thine only Son, our Saviour Jesus
Christ. Amen[11]

Lord, bid me come to you across the waters.

Ri Traghad	The ebb
's ri lionadh . . .	and the flow . . .
Mar a bha	as it was
Mar a tha	as it is
Mar a bhitheas	as it shall be
Gu bruth	evermore
Ri traghad	the ebb
's ri lionadh	and the flow[12]

Notes

NOTES

TIDES AND SEASONS

1 Gerard Manley Hopkins, 'Heaven-Haven'
2 Arthur Hugh Clough, 'Say Not the Struggle Naught Availeth'
3 H. J. Massingham, *The Tree of Life*, Chapman and Hall 1943
4 Gerard Manley Hopkins, 'God's Grandeur'

INCOMING TIDE

1 T. S. Eliot, 'Burnt Norton', *Four Quartets*, Faber 1959
2 Pierre Teilhard de Chardin, *Hymn of the Universe*, Fontana 1969
3 The 'ninefold welcome' of the newly born by the Aid Woman immersing the child in the awareness of the Holy Three; and often in the inflowing tide
4 G. S. Walker (Ed.), *Sancti Columbani Opera*, in series *Scriptores Latini Hiberniae* Vol. 2, Dublin Institute for Advanced Studies, 1959
5 Julian of Norwich, *Revelations of Divine Love*
6 G. R. D. McLean, *Poems of the Western Highlanders*, SPCK 1961, p. 275. Also in McLean, *Praying with Highland Christians*, Triangle 1988, p. 11
7 *Poems of the Western Highlanders*, p. 75

FULL TIDE

1 *Julius Caesar*, Act iv, scene ii
2 Ignatius Loyola, *Spiritual Exercises* (trs. Thomas Corbishley, sj), Anthony Clarke, 1979
3 For the meaning of *Caim*, the 'encircling prayer', see p. 105
4 Robin Flower, *Irish Tradition*, Clarendon Press 1947, p. 42
5 *Poems of the Western Highlanders*, p. 59; *Praying with Highland Christians*, p. 28
6 Traditional Gaelic prayer, translated by G. R. D. McLean and quoted in Martin Reith, *God in our Midst*, SPCK 1975, p. 33

EBB TIDE

1   *Hamlet*, Act ii, scene ii
2   Quoted in Ruth Etchells, *Unafraid to Be*, IVP 1969
3   Alistair Maclean, *Hebridean Altars*, Edinburgh 1937, p. 95
4   ibid., p. 60
5   T. S. Eliot, *The Elder Statesman*, Faber 1959
6   John 3.16
7   Isaiah 41.10
8   see David Adam, *The Edge of Glory*, Triangle 1985, p. 76
9   *Hebridean Altars*, p. 152
10 *The Book of Common Prayer*, Collect for the 15th Sunday after Trinity.

LOW TIDE

1   D. H. Lawrence, *Complete Poems*, William Heinemann Ltd., 1957, Vol. 3, p. 174
2   David Gascoyne, *Collected Poems*, Oxford University Press 1965
3   *Hebridean Altars*, p. 142
4   ibid., p. 122
5   ibid., p. 89
6   John 21.4
7   Kevin Crossley-Holland, *The Anglo-Saxon World*, Oxford University Press 1900, p. 53
8   *Hebridean Altars*, p. 131
9   ibid., p. 55
10 ibid., p. 47
11 *The Book of Common Prayer*, Collect for Evening Prayer
12 Fiona Macleod, *The Winged Destiny*, William Heinemann Ltd. 1927, p. 103

THE CRY OF THE DEER

Meditations on the Hymn of St Patrick

by David Adam

Following the popularity of *The Edge of Glory*, David Adam continues to explore the Celtic way of prayer.

The Cry of the Deer takes us deeper into the prayer experience through a series of meditations leading into practical exercises in affirming the Presence of God through prayer. These meditations are based on the eternal certainties of the Christian faith, as acclaimed in the translation of the Hymn of St Patrick known as 'The Deer's Cry'. They are designed to help us to experience faith not merely as creeds but as a vital, living relationship with God which touches every aspect of our lives.

Praying with
HIGHLAND CHRISTIANS

G. R. D. McLean

Foreword by Sally Magnusson

A selection of prayers from G. R. D. McLean's translations of traditional Gaelic poems, *Poems of the Western Highlanders*. Though they arise out of a social structure now largely vanished, they deal with the unchanging basics of human life – with bodily needs, the daily round, family love, our fears and temptations and the need for security.

'A refreshing reminder of the great riches of our own heritage . . . Page after page vibrates with a 'glory' which for many has passed away from the earth.'
David Adam

'It is a privilege to pray with these Celtic Christians. Their conversations with the God they loved all those years ago must surely enhance our own, just as their humanity and their faith can only enlarge ours.'
Sally Magnusson